Say Goodbye to Being Shy

A Workbook to Help Kids Overcome Shyness

RICHARD BROZOVICH, PH.D.
LINDA CHASE, LMSW

Instant Help Books
A Division of New Harbinger Publications, Inc.

Publisher's Note

Distributed in Canada by Raincoast Books

Copyright © 2008 by Richard Brozovich and Linda Chase
          Instant Help Books
          A Division of New Harbinger Publications, Inc.
          5674 Shattuck Avenue
          Oakland, CA 94609
          www.newharbinger.com

Cover design by Amy Shoup
Illustrations by Steve Barr

Cover photo is a model used for illustrative purposes only.

Library of Congress publication data on file with publisher

16   15   14

10   9   8   7   6   5   4   3

*To all the children we have worked with
who have taught us so much about overcoming shyness*

Acknowledgments

We gratefully acknowledge all of the people who have contributed to the creation of this book. We would especially like to thank:

Doug Chase, whose valuable suggestions and editing skills have contributed significantly to the clarity of this book

Karen Brozovich, whose creative ideas were incorporated into the book

The Brozovich grandchildren, who provided explanations of what it is like to be shy as a child

Our spouses, Diane Brozovich and Karl Chase, who continue to provide encouragement and unfailing support

Contents

To Parents

Shyness is very common among children. More than one in three adults say that they were shy at some time during their childhood. Many parents think that their children will outgrow their shyness, but if your child has had noticeable periods of shyness for more than six months, then shyness has likely become a pattern of behavior, and this is definitely a pattern you will want to break.

It is not fun to be shy. I know this very well, because I was a shy child and teen myself. I didn't like to speak in class, I hated to meet new people, and I didn't have many friends because I was too shy to reach out to other children. I did not learn to overcome my shyness until I was in my mid-twenties. Even now, although many people would consider me an extrovert, I still feel like a shy person inside. I wouldn't wish this on anyone, and I'm sure you feel the same.

Most shy children show very early signs of anxiety and hypervigilance when they are very young—just a few months old. Scientists tell us that there is a gene for shyness, and that if children are born with this gene, their brains are wired to react with more anxiety and fear than children who do not have this gene.

The good news is that children can learn the emotional, social, and behavioral skills to overcome their genetic predisposition to shyness, and the earlier that they do this, the better. In fact, studies using standard tests of behavior and personality suggest that children who are taught skills to overcome their shyness at an early age cannot be distinguished from children who were never shy.

The activities in this book have been used by the authors to help countless children overcome their shyness. They will teach your child to self-calm and relax in the face of anxiety or fear, to master the basic skills of social interaction like making eye contact and smiling, and to change negative self-critical thoughts into positive ones.

All of the activities in the book will benefit your child—and may benefit you too if you are a shy person! However, some children may need extra help. There is a thin line where shyness crosses over into an anxiety disorder, and you should not hesitate to seek professional guidance if you feel that your child has crossed this line. If you feel that your child's shyness keeps him from normal, age-appropriate activities, such as joining a team or club, or going over to another kid's home for a play date, then you should certainly seek out a professional counselor. This workbook will still be of tremendous value as a way to reinforce the skills that your child is learning in counseling.

As you help your child, you will probably find out that it is difficult for him to talk about certain issues. Never force your child to talk if he doesn't want to. The best way to get children to open up is to be a good role model. Talk about your thoughts, feelings, and experiences as they relate to each activity, stressing the positive ways that *you* cope with problems. Even if your child doesn't say a thing back, your words will have an impact on his behavior.

There is no wrong way to use this workbook to help your child, as long as you remain patient and respectful of your child's feelings. If your child is being seen by a counselor, make sure you share this workbook with the therapist. She may have some additional ideas on how best to use the activities.

Shyness can be a lifelong problem, but I know that this workbook can help prevent this from happening to your child. Your patience and understanding will make all the difference.

Sincerely,

Lawrence E. Shapiro, Ph.D.

Using *Say Goodbye to Being Shy*
Ten Tips for Parents and Counselors

1. **Encourage practice.**
   Remind children that the activities will be most beneficial when they are practiced on a regular basis. Reading this workbook will not change behavior; practicing will.

2. **Encourage record keeping.**
   Help children develop systems to track the times they practice new skills. Use charts or graphs to record their efforts. Keeping records will give children proof of their progress, which can be especially helpful when they are feeling discouraged.

3. **Reinforce desired behavior.**
   Using the system described in Activity 1: Your Reward List, record the points and provide the rewards children have earned. Use specific praise to reinforce behavior; instead of saying, "Good girl" or "Good job," say, "You did a good job of ordering your own food just now."

4. **Be a role model.**
   Show children that adults also need to put forth effort to change their behavior. Think of your successes in overcoming problems or your struggles with new challenges, and share appropriate experiences with children.

5. **Be a cheerleader.**
   Provide gentle encouragement for children to try behaviors that they perceive as difficult, but avoid the temptation to overwhelm them with suggestions. State any advice briefly and in a positive way, for example, "That was a good response! Let's do it again, and this time, try making eye contact while you say it." Avoid criticism, and make it a personal rule to offer eight unconditional positive comments before making one suggestion for improvement.

6. **Play a role.**
   Assume the role of someone to whom children react with shyness, for example, a teacher that a child is having difficulty with. Enthusiastically role-play responses with the child, trying to provide a realistic experience by being like the actual person.

7. **Provide dress rehearsals.**
   To prepare children for a new experience, try a "dress rehearsal." Make practice realistic by changing your appearance and adding props, when possible. It will help if children can visit the actual location ahead of time. For example,

for children invited to a skating party, arrange a visit to the rink. Give them opportunities to rehearse some of the behaviors they would be likely to engage in at the party.

8. **Ask questions.**
Get children's answers to important questions such as these:

   - What would help as you work on this new skill?
   - What could I do that would help you the most?
   - What could your teacher do that would make a difference?
   - Who else can help?

9. **Be patient.**
Remember that developing self-confidence and assertiveness is a gradual, difficult task for children with a history of shy behaviors. Allow them to set the pace of progress. Through your words and behavior, demonstrate the kind of patience that you hope they will have with themselves.

10. **Envision success.**
In your mind, see children as self-assured and assertive. Imagine scenarios in which their shyness is gone and they are interacting in a relaxed, confident manner. As you develop this mental image, your attitude and body language will convey your belief to them in subtle but powerful ways. You will be seeing possibilities in them that they cannot see yet and creating the hope they need to become successful.

Note: The activities in the book follow a planned sequence. By completing the activities in order, children will be able to develop skills that facilitate the learning of subsequent behavior. Unless specific situations warrant doing some activities out of order, we suggest that the activities be completed in the sequence presented.

A Message to Young Readers

Hi! It is very exciting that you are going to say goodbye to being shy. The activities in this book have helped other people, and they will help you, too.

Shyness is a way of feeling afraid. This feeling can keep you from having a happy life. It can stop you from having fun with your family and friends and it can keep you from meeting new people. How can you get rid of this feeling that causes so much trouble? That's what this book is about. It is full of activities that will help you say goodbye to being shy. Lots of these activities are fun, and you will be able to try many new things.

Starting today, don't think of yourself as a shy person. Instead, think of yourself as a person who acts shy some of the time. Imagine how things will be when you are no longer shy. Picture yourself laughing and talking with other people, making new friends, and having fun. As you work on the activities in this book, imagine this often. It will make the shyness go away sooner. Before you know it, the good things you have been imagining will become true for you.

Each time you do one of the activities, you will get a little less shy. As you do more activities, you will become a lot less shy. And if you do many of the activities, you will say goodbye to being shy—and hello to more fun and more friends. As the shyness goes away, you will be able to start doing things you have never done before. Maybe you will sleep over at a friend's house for the first time or go to a birthday party or read for your class. As you become more confident, all of these things can be fun for you.

Many of the activities involve writing. It does not matter if you do the writing or if somebody else listens to your answers and writes them for you. The important part is that you think about the answers. Your answers should be written in the book, but it is okay if someone else writes them.

You will be asked to do different things, and if you do them in order, they might be a little hard (but not too hard). Take one step at a time, and you will be able to do them. Your parent or counselor can help, too.

It's time to get started!

Sincerely,

Richard Brozovich
Linda Chase

About This Activity

You will develop a list of rewards that provide an extra reason to work on activities. By using rewards from others to improve your performance, you can learn to work hard to achieve your goals.

Many times, people work hard because they enjoy what they are doing. It may make them feel good, or they may know that their hard work will pay off in the future. And sometimes, people work harder if they know that they will get a special reward when the work is finished.

For each activity you do in this book, you can earn reward points. The book suggests how many points you can earn for each activity. In this activity, you and your parent or counselor will make a list of rewards you can receive for earning those points. The rewards should be things you really want and things your parent is happy to give you. They should be special things you do not receive all the time. You and your parent will have to agree on how many points are needed for each reward on your list.

Here is a sample of a reward list completed by Bill and his dad. Remember, these are things Bill really wanted, and his dad was happy to give him. Your parent may not agree with some of these rewards, or you may not want some of the rewards Bill wants. You and your parent have to figure out a reward list just for you.

Reward	Points Required
Treat at ice cream shop	35
$5 to spend at the hobby shop	90
Stay up an extra half-hour	20
Rent a movie or game of my choice	45
Thirty minutes playing games with Dad	45
New mountain bike	1400
Skip one day of chores	30

On the next page, you'll find space to make your own reward list. You can add to the list or change it at any time, but you and your parent must agree to the change.

A Workbook to Help Kids Overcome Shyness

My Reward List

Reward　　　　　　　　　　　　　　　　　　　　　　**Points Required**

_____　　　_____

_____　　　_____

_____　　　_____

_____　　　_____

_____　　　_____

_____　　　_____

_____　　　_____

_____　　　_____

_____　　　_____

_____　　　_____

_____　　　_____

_____　　_____
Your parent's signature　　　　　　　　　　　Date

_____　　_____
Your signature　　　　　　　　　　　　　　　Date

To use the reward list, you and your parent must keep a record of your points earned and points spent. Here is a sample of Bill's record.

Date	Points Earned	Reward and Points Spent	Points Left to Spend
Oct. 1	5	0	5
Oct. 2	8	0	13
Oct. 3	7	0	20
Oct. 4	12	0	32
Oct. 5	0	0	32
Oct. 6	10	0	42
Oct. 7	12	Ice Cream - 35	19
Oct. 8	14	0	33
Oct. 9	15	0	48
Oct. 10	12	0	60

Notice that when Bill spent points for a trip to the ice cream shop, those points were subtracted from the Points Left to Spend column.

On the next page, you can start your own record of reward points. Before you start, make extra copies so that you will always have a blank record. Using the reward list and keeping records will give you extra reasons to work on activities every day.

My Reward List

Reward — Points Required

Your parent's signature — Date

Your signature — Date

Reward Points
5 points for reading this activity
5 points for completing My Reward List

A Workbook to Help Kids Overcome Shyness

My Reward Points

Date	Points Earned	Reward and Points Spent	Points Left to Spend
____	_____	_____	_____
____	_____	_____	_____
____	_____	_____	_____
____	_____	_____	_____
____	_____	_____	_____
____	_____	_____	_____
____	_____	_____	_____
____	_____	_____	_____
____	_____	_____	_____
____	_____	_____	_____
____	_____	_____	_____
____	_____	_____	_____

Say Goodbye to Being Shy

About This Activity

You will learn that most people act shy in some situations and that acting shy is a normal reaction. You will also find out that you can learn how to handle feeling shy by practicing what works for you.

Many famous people have felt and acted shy. One famous person who worked hard to become more self-confident is the former president of the United States, Jimmy Carter. President Carter had to be brave and strong to overcome feelings of shyness. It would have been easier for President Carter to stay at home on his farm, but he was determined not to let feelings of shyness control his life. You can be like President Carter. You can practice and work hard and achieve your own goal.

Sometimes, grownups forget how it feels to be a child who acts shy. Following are the words of two children who each remember a time when they felt shy and what they did about it. Here is what they said in their own words—their own spelling and punctuation, too!

My Shy Moments: Rachel (age 10)

I get shy when somebody asks me a questin (someone I don't know to well, my stomach feels empty. I feel like I am floating away. I am so light. When that happens I count to ten take a deep breath think of an answer and say it in my mind and tell them my answer.

My Shy Moments: Elizabeth (age 9)

My river dance recital. How did I help myself? Breathe count to 10—pretend everyone is in their underwear—and just do what you have to do! go out there and show those people what you are made of!

Both of these children had no problem thinking of times when they felt shy. Notice that each picked a different situation and had a different way of handling shy feelings. While almost half of all children describe themselves as feeling shy, each of them feels it in their own way. You will find that some ideas for handling your shy feelings work well for you, and others do not. The important thing is that you continue to try new ideas and practice those that work best for you.

In your own words, describe some of your shy moments, just as Rachel and Elizabeth did. Tell how you tried to deal with feeling shy.

My Shy Moments

by _____

Shy moment 1: _____

_____

_____

How I tried to deal with feeling shy: _____

_____

_____

_____

_____

Shy moment 2: _____

_____

_____

How I tried to deal with feeling shy: _____

_____

_____

_____

_____

Shy moment 3: _____

_____

_____

How I tried to deal with feeling shy: _____

_____

_____

_____

If you have a favorite way to fight shyness, write it here: _____

_____

_____

_____

Reward Points
5 points for reading this activity
2 points for writing one shy moment
2 more points for writing each additional shy moment
2 points for writing a favorite way to fight shyness

What Does Your Shyness Feel Like?

About This Activity

Shyness feels different to different people. In this activity, you will have a chance to think about how shyness feels to you. You will also draw a picture to show how big your shyness feels now. At the end of this book, you will draw another picture that will show you how much progress you have made.

Keep practicing what works for you!

Feeling shy is not fun. Check any of the things that happen to you when you are feeling shy:

☐ My head hurts.

☐ My stomach hurts.

☐ My heart beats faster.

☐ I get warm.

☐ My face turns red.

☐ I get short of breath.

☐ My mouth feels dry.

☐ I have trouble swallowing.

☐ My muscles get tight.

☐ I feel tired.

☐ I feel grouchy.

☐ I feel sad.

☐ I feel scared or worried.

☐ I feel shaky or restless.

☐ I avoid eye contact.

☐ I feel like hiding.

☐ I have trouble falling asleep or staying asleep.

☐ I have trouble paying attention.

☐ I feel afraid of other people.

☐ I feel like other people are staring at me.

☐ I feel afraid to talk or ask for help.

☐ I freeze and just do nothing.

Doing the activities in this book will help you get rid of the shyness and replace it with fun, friends, and laughter. In the box below, draw a picture of yourself and the shyness. Draw the shyness as a circle in the middle of your body. Does your shyness feel as big as

a quarter,   your stomach,   your whole body,

or does it feel even bigger than you are?

Add today's date so you will know when you drew this.

By doing the activities in this book, you will feel more confident and relaxed most of the time. You will feel happier and friendlier, with more friends and more fun than ever before. The shyness will get smaller and smaller.

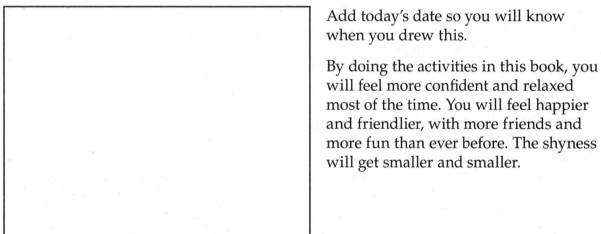

Reward Points
3 points for reading this activity
3 points for completing the checklist
3 points for drawing a picture

Activity 4

The Turtle Who Learned How to Stick His Neck Out

About This Activity

You will learn that everyone reacts to things around them in their own way. Some people have learned to react in ways that are not helpful to them. For shy and anxious people, this can mean that harmless situations often make them feel frightened or nervous.

The sun sparkled on the calm, blue pond as three little ducks paddled through the water. Fred, the shy turtle, poked his nose out of the water. When Fred saw the ducks, he dove back under the water and returned to his home, where he felt safe.

Fred's brothers and sisters also saw the ducks and were curious. They swam to the ducks and played with them. When they went home, they told Fred how much fun they had had with the ducks. Fred was puzzled. Why was he afraid when his brothers and sisters were not?

Later, Fred decided to swim to the shore and lie in the sun with his brothers and sisters. He felt comfortable and happy as the sun warmed his shell. With his head and arms inside the shell, Fred felt safe.

"Ribbit, ribbit." What was that noise? Fred was interested but didn't want to stick his neck out because he was afraid. Then he heard splashing. What was going on? After a while, Fred was so curious that he poked his head out—just a little. There were his brothers and sisters, playing with some frogs! They were jumping off a log into the pond. Then they gave the frogs a ride through the water while the frogs sat on their backs. It looked like fun, but Fred didn't try it. He was afraid that he wouldn't be able to climb onto the log without falling.

That evening, Fred was home alone, thinking about the fun he had missed. He felt sad and wished he could be braver. There was a knock at the door; it was Fred's Uncle Walter. Uncle Walter was the oldest and wisest turtle at the pond. As soon as he came in, Uncle Walter could see that Fred was sad.

Say Goodbye to Being Shy

"What's the matter, Freddie?" said Uncle Walter. Fred loved and trusted his uncle. He knew that Uncle Walter loved him. Before Fred could speak, he felt turtle tears running down his cheek. Uncle Walter picked him up, hugged him, and said, "You're a terrific turtle. Now tell your Uncle Walter what is wrong."

"I don't know why I'm always so afraid," said Fred. "I'm just not like other turtles."

"Well," said Uncle Walter, "remember that nobody is born brave. Because turtles have shells, it's very easy for them to keep their necks and heads inside, where it is safe. We have to learn that sometimes it's okay to stick our necks out. You know, Freddie, there are other old turtles who kept themselves safe but missed a lot of fun in life because they would not stick their necks out."

"But how can I know when it's safe or when to take a chance?" said Fred. "How can I learn to be brave?"

"You are brave," said Uncle Walter, "because you had the courage to tell me about something that wasn't easy to tell. You and I can work together so that you will be able to stick your neck out and start taking little chances. Gradually you will learn, just as I did, that to join in the fun of life, you must learn when it's okay to come out of your shell. Learning it will require bravery, patience, and hard work. Are you willing to try it?"

"Oh, yes," said Fred. "I want to learn to be just like you when I'm a grown-up turtle."

Thinking about Fred's story, write the answers to the following questions. If you need help, ask your parent or counselor.

What do people mean when they say that someone was willing to stick his neck out?

_____

_____

Do you think that some turtles stick their necks out more than others do? Why? What good things happen to turtles who are willing to stick their necks out?

_____

_____

What did Uncle Walter mean when he said, "… nobody is born brave"?

_____

_____

Uncle Walter said he would teach Fred to start taking little chances. Why do you think Uncle Walter wanted to start with little chances?

_____

_____

What little chances do you think Fred can take to practice being brave?

_____

_____

> ### *Reward Points*
> **5 points for reading this activity**
> **2 points for each written answer**

About This Activity

You will learn that people are brave in their own ways. Thinking about bravery will help you get ready to do more brave things.

Did you know that you do brave things every day? Perhaps you feel a little afraid about getting on the school bus each day, but you do it. Maybe the cafeteria at school seems noisy and scary, but you make yourself go there. People face many challenges every day and have to decide whether to meet those challenges or avoid them. Everyone is brave in different ways, and what is easy for some is hard for others.

One way to be brave is to do the right thing, even when you feel afraid. If you feel afraid to talk in front of the class and do it anyway, you are being brave. If you feel afraid to say hello to a new student and do it anyway, you are being brave. Right after you do something brave, stop and notice how you feel. Isn't that a great feeling?

Think about people who have become heroes by making themselves do brave things. A baseball player may not have made the team as a child but kept trying until he became great at his sport. A girl who was teased for her actions was a hero because she still kept doing what she knew was right. Whatever the situation, a hero always does something brave before becoming great. Each time you read a book about a famous hero, remember to look for the ways that person acted brave.

Interview

Using the questions below, ask a teenager or grownup to tell you about a time that he or she was brave.

Name of person _____

What brave thing did you do? _____

_____

_____

When did it happen? _____

How were you able to do this brave thing even though you felt afraid?

_____

_____

_____

_____

How did you feel afterward?

_____

_____

A Time You Were Brave

Think about your life. Choose a time when you were brave and write about it below.

What you did:

_____

_____

When it happened: _____

How were you able to do this brave thing?

_____

_____

_____

_____

How you felt afterward:

_____

_____

Reward Points
5 points for reading this activity
5 points for completing the interview
3 points for writing about a time you were brave

Activity 6   Practicing Bravery

About This Activity

This activity will help you think about doing more brave acts. Practicing being brave can help you become a braver person.

There is a wonderful thing about being brave: the more you practice being brave, the easier it gets. For example, if you are afraid to swim, the fear gets smaller each time you go for a swimming lesson. With every lesson, it gets a little easier.

Choose a time when you will practice being brave and write your plan below.

What you will do:

_____

_____

When it will be: _____

Where it will be: _____

How will you be able to do the brave thing?

_____

_____

_____

_____

_____

Say Goodbye to Being Shy

The Brave Acts List

Congratulations—you are turning yourself into a brave person! That's very important, because the world needs brave people.

Once you have done the brave act you just planned, you can start a Brave Acts List. On the first line of the list, write down the brave thing you did and the date you did it. Each time you do another brave act, write it down.

Below is Fred the Turtle's list. Even if other turtles didn't see the brave things Fred did, he knew what he had done. And even if other people don't notice your brave act, you will know that you have been brave. When you have finished your list, it will show you that you are turning into one of the brave people in the world. Way to go!

Fred's Brave Acts List	
I felt afraid, but I was able to ask Uncle Walter for help.	June 16
When no one was looking, I swam up to the climbing log.	June 18
I practiced climbing on the log with my front feet.	June 20
I answered the phone in a strong voice and said, "Hello, Turtle Home. This is Fred speaking."	June 22
I practiced balancing on the log with all four feet.	June 23
I tried to climb all the way onto the log. I fell off seven times, but I kept trying.	June 25
For the first time, I went by myself to Turtle Beach, all the way on the other side of the pond.	June 27
I went with my brothers and sisters, even though I knew they were going to meet the frogs by the climbing log.	June 28
I climbed onto the log in front of everyone. I fell off twice, but I kept trying and I made it to the top.	June 30
I invited a frog to sit on my back as I paddled around the pond.	July 2

A Workbook to Help Kids Overcome Shyness

My Brave Acts List

What I Did   **Date**

_____   _____

_____   _____

_____   _____

_____   _____

_____   _____

_____   _____

_____   _____

_____   _____

_____   _____

_____   _____

Reward Points
5 points for reading this activity
3 points for writing about your next brave act
2 points for each item on My Brave Acts List

Breathing Calmness In and Shyness Out

Activity 7

About This Activity

You will learn a way to breathe that can help you feel calm and relaxed. When you feel calm and relaxed, you are less likely to act shy.

Notice how you are breathing. You probably breathe in a little bit of air and then blow it out. But your body can hold a lot more air than that, so it is possible for you to breathe in and out a lot more air than you normally do.

Pretend you are blowing into a balloon and start to blow out air. Keep blowing out until your stomach muscles start to feel tight. You will be getting rid of lots of old, stale air. Then relax and breathe in deeply. Notice how your body fills up with just the right amount of air.

As you slowly blow out the old air, think, "Now I am blowing out all the shyness and fear." As your body fills with fresh air, think, "Now I am filling up with calmness." Try doing this two or three times. Those slow, deep breaths will make your whole body more relaxed and calm. When your body is calmer, your mind will start to feel calmer, too. Try it—it works!

You can use this exercise whenever you want to feel more relaxed and think more clearly. Circle the times when you think that deep breathing can help you. Add your own ideas on the blank lines.

Before a test

When I'm feeling shy

Before recess

Just before it's my turn at bat

When I'm going to meet new people

When I'm trying to fall asleep

Before I need to read in class

At lunch

Just before I start a race

_____

_____

_____

_____

_____

_____

_____

_____

Reward Points

5 points for reading this activity

**2 points for circling items
(no matter how many are circled)**

1 point for each blank line filled

Relaxing Your Muscles   Activity 8

About This Activity

You will learn how to use muscle relaxation as a way to achieve peaceful feelings.

Now that you know how to use breathing to become more relaxed, you are ready to learn another way to relax your body and mind. Relaxing can help when you don't feel good, when you are trying to fall asleep, and when you feel worried or afraid. As with other skills, every time you practice this exercise, you will get better at it. You will be able to relax yourself more and more quickly.

First, practice knowing the difference between tense muscles and relaxed muscles. Put your hands together and push. Feel how your arm muscles tense. Stop pushing and feel how your muscles relax. Now tense all the muscles in your face. Use your hand to feel, or a mirror to see, the way your face becomes tense. Stop tensing your face and feel how the muscles relax.

Now you are ready to practice relaxing all your muscles. Find a comfortable place to sit or lie down. Get your body quiet and start to think about your feet, including your toes and ankles. Concentrate on this area of your body and say to yourself very slowly, "My feet are relaxing. My feet are relaxing. My feet are relaxed." As you slowly say this to yourself, make your feet, your toes, and your ankles feel calm by relaxing the muscles in them. You can pretend your feet are ice cubes slowly melting into the ground.

Next, think about your legs. As you concentrate on your legs, very slowly say to yourself, "My legs are relaxing. My legs are relaxing. My legs are relaxed." Now, with your feet and legs relaxed, move up to your hips. Concentrate on the area of your hips and think to yourself, "My hips are relaxing. My hips are relaxing. My hips are relaxed."

Slowly move up to your waist area, including your stomach and lower back. Relax this part of your body in the same way. Now think about your chest and upper back and relax these areas of your body.

Next, concentrate on your shoulders, arms, and hands. Slowly repeat to yourself, "My shoulders, arms, and hands are relaxing. My shoulders, arms, and hands are relaxing. My shoulders, arms, and hands are relaxed."

Now that the rest of your body is relaxed, all that is left are your neck, face, and head. Concentrate on these parts, and pay particular attention to your eyes and tongue because these parts are often hard to relax. Say, "My neck, face, and head are relaxing. My neck, face, and head are relaxing. My neck, face, and head are relaxed."

Once all the parts of your body have relaxed, stay quiet and notice how this feels. You are doing a very powerful thing, because as you relax your muscles, everything about your body is getting more relaxed.

Being quiet and relaxed this way is good for your body and your mind. When you are relaxed, it is easier for your body to stay healthy and easier for your mind to think of wonderful, creative new ideas. If you practice relaxation often, you will find that you get more relaxed more quickly. It is a great skill that will help you all your life. Each time you practice this exercise, write down the date, time, and where you practiced.

Date   **Time**   **Place**

_____   _____   _____

_____   _____   _____

_____   _____   _____

_____   _____   _____

_____   _____   _____

_____   _____   _____

Reward Points

**10 points for reading this activity and practicing
the tense-relax training the first time**

**4 points each time you practice and record
the date, time, and place**

About This Activity

You will learn that music can help put you in a positive mood. When feelings of shyness bother you, the right music can help you feel more relaxed and confident.

When you listen to a song, stop and think about how it makes you feel. Does the music make you feel happy or sad? Angry or calm? Like dancing?

Each time you listen to a song, write its name below. Then write how that song made you feel. Notice that different kinds of music bring up different feelings in you.

The Song I Listened To   **How It Made Me Feel**

_____   _____

_____   _____

_____   _____

_____   _____

_____   _____

_____   _____

_____   _____

_____   _____

Now think about which music can help create certain feelings in you. Try different types of music until you find what works best for you.

When I want to concentrate, I can listen to _____.

When I want to cheer up, I can listen to _____.

When I want to feel more relaxed, I can listen to _____.

When I want to feel confident, I can listen to _____.

Reward Points

3 points for reading this activity

1 point for each song you pair with a feeling

1 point for each music choice you make

About This Activity

You will learn how to use your imagination to stop scary dreams. People who take action to stop scary dreams are not acting shy!

If you ever have bad dreams, and especially if you have had the same bad dream more than once, this exercise can help. First, think about what happens in your dream. Then, think about how you would like the dream to end. If your bad dream is about being chased, you might pretend you had huge rolls of magic tape and could tape up the one who is chasing you. If your bad dream is about falling, you might imagine having superpowers so that you could fly away to keep from getting hurt. In the space below, draw a picture that shows how you would like your bad dream to end.

Many times, when people imagine happy endings for their scary dreams, those dreams stop. If your scary dream does not stop after doing this the first time, draw a second picture that shows how you would like it to end. This time, use more detail and more color.

Making Eye Contact

About This Activity

This activity will help you practice making eye contact with other people. Making eye contact is an important skill for getting along with others. As you do this activity, you will also be learning an important way to practice new behaviors.

To become skilled at making eye contact, you need to learn how to look at other people's eyes without staring or glaring at them. Positive eye contact should last for just a second or two before you move your eyes away. If you're not sure how to make positive eye contact, ask your parent or counselor to practice with you and tell you when you do it just right. As you practice, you will get better at it.

On a scale from 0 to 10, rate the following types of people by how hard it is for you to make eye contact with them.

← **Easier**   **Harder** →

Adults I don't know	0	1	2	3	4	5	6	7	8	9	10
Boys who are close friends	0	1	2	3	4	5	6	7	8	9	10
Girls who are close friends	0	1	2	3	4	5	6	7	8	9	10
Teachers I know well	0	1	2	3	4	5	6	7	8	9	10
Other teachers	0	1	2	3	4	5	6	7	8	9	10
The school secretary	0	1	2	3	4	5	6	7	8	9	10
The principal of my school	0	1	2	3	4	5	6	7	8	9	10
Girls I don't know	0	1	2	3	4	5	6	7	8	9	10
Boys I don't know	0	1	2	3	4	5	6	7	8	9	10
My mother	0	1	2	3	4	5	6	7	8	9	10
My father	0	1	2	3	4	5	6	7	8	9	10

	← Easier					Harder →				
My brother(s)	0	1	2	3	4	5	6	7	8	9	10
My sister(s)	0	1	2	3	4	5	6	7	8	9	10
Relatives I see often	0	1	2	3	4	5	6	7	8	9	10
Relatives I don't see often	0	1	2	3	4	5	6	7	8	9	10
Classmates (boys)	0	1	2	3	4	5	6	7	8	9	10
Classmates (girls)	0	1	2	3	4	5	6	7	8	9	10

Add any people in your life who are not on the list, and rate them as well:

_____	0	1	2	3	4	5	6	7	8	9	10
_____	0	1	2	3	4	5	6	7	8	9	10
_____	0	1	2	3	4	5	6	7	8	9	10
_____	0	1	2	3	4	5	6	7	8	9	10
_____	0	1	2	3	4	5	6	7	8	9	10
_____	0	1	2	3	4	5	6	7	8	9	10

Next, you are going to use your list with ratings to make a new list showing the people you just rated, in order from easiest to hardest. Below is a sample of such a list prepared by Amanda. She used her opinion to rate her sister as easiest, her brother and mom next easiest, and so on.

Amanda's List of Eye Contact From Easiest to Hardest

People	How Hard It Is to Make Eye Contact
My sister	0
My brother	1
Mom	1
Dad	2
Grandma	2
My friend Joan	2
My friend Susan	3
Girls in class	5
Aunt Mary, Aunt Fran	5
Girls I don't know	6
Other relatives	6
My teacher	6
Other teachers	7
School secretary	7
Boys in class	8
Boys I don't know	9
Principal	9
Adults I don't know	10

Now you are ready to make your own list from easiest to hardest.

People   **How Hard It Is
                                                             to Make Eye Contact**

_____   _____

_____   _____

_____   _____

_____   _____

_____   _____

_____   _____

_____   _____

_____   _____

_____   _____

_____   _____

_____   _____

_____   _____

_____   _____

People	How Hard It Is to Make Eye Contact
_____	_____
_____	_____
_____	_____
_____	_____
_____	_____
_____	_____
_____	_____
_____	_____
_____	_____
_____	_____
_____	_____
_____	_____
_____	_____
_____	_____

Once your list is finished, you are ready to practice. Start with the people you rated as easiest. As you practice making eye contact with them, you will begin to feel more confident in your ability to make positive eye contact with others.

After you feel comfortable and confident making eye contact with the easiest group of people, it is time to move one position down on your list, to someone you rated as just a little harder. When you feel confident with that person, move down your list to a person you rated as even harder. Continue practicing this way until you have gained the confidence to make eye contact with anyone on your list.

Use the space below to keep a record of your progress. The chart has seven days for practice at each level, but you can use as many days as you need. If you want to practice more than seven days at a certain level, just keep your record on a separate sheet for the extra days.

Difficulty Level for Eye Contact	Date	People with Whom I Made Eye Contact
	_____	_____
	_____	_____
0-1-2	_____	_____
(easier)	_____	_____
	_____	_____
	_____	_____
	_____	_____

Once you have practiced and are ready, move to the next level.

Difficulty Level for Eye Contact	Date	People with Whom I Made Eye Contact
	_____	_____
	_____	_____
3-4	_____	_____
(little harder)	_____	_____
	_____	_____
	_____	_____
	_____	_____

You have been practicing making eye contact that you thought might be a little more difficult. When you are ready, try the next level.

Difficulty Level for Eye Contact	Date	People with Whom I Made Eye Contact
	_____	_____
	_____	_____
5-6-7	_____	_____
(harder)	_____	_____
	_____	_____
	_____	_____
	_____	_____

You must be feeling great about how much progress you have made. Aren't you surprising yourself by how strong you are? It's time to work on the last part of your list.

Difficulty Level for Eye Contact	Date	People with Whom I Made Eye Contact
	_____	_____
	_____	_____
8-9-10	_____	_____
(hardest)	_____	_____
	_____	_____
	_____	_____
	_____	_____

When you have practiced this part of the list, good for you!

You have just used an important way to practice new behaviors. It can help you overcome feeling nervous in most situations. Here are the five steps to follow:

Step 1

Make a list, starting with the times when the behavior is easiest and ending with the times when it is hardest. List as many steps—from easiest to hardest—as you can.

Step 2

Start by practicing the behavior when it is easiest. Continue practicing the behavior until you feel comfortable and confident.

Step 3

Keep a daily record of your practice.

Step 4

Try the next-hardest example of the behavior on your list. Again, practice at this level of difficulty until you feel comfortable and confident. If you find you cannot do the behavior at one level, go back and practice more at an easier level. When you are ready, try the harder behavior again. Once you feel comfortable and confident, try an even harder behavior. Keep doing this until you are comfortable and confident at the level of difficulty you want to reach.

Step 5

Continue practicing the behavior until it becomes a habit.

> ### Reward Points
> **8 points for reading this activity**
> **5 points for doing the rating chart**
> **1 point for each person added to the rating chart**
> **5 points for completing the list of people from easiest to hardest to make eye contact with**
> **2 points for each day you record eye contact**

About This Activity

You will learn that you tell others important things even when you are not speaking. Other people look at your body language to try to figure out how you feel and how you might act. The exercises in this activity will show you how to use friendly body language and make it easier for you to make new friends.

On the line below each picture, write whether the person looks sad, angry, afraid, or happy.

_____   _____

_____   _____

Even when you can't hear people speaking, you can tell how they feel because of the way their faces look and the way they hold their arms, legs, and bodies. This is called body language.

Your body language tells other people how you feel, too. To practice showing your feelings, write each of these words on a separate piece of paper:

Afraid	Angry
Interested	Kind
Confused	Sad
Embarrassed	Friendly
Calm	Surprised
Anxious	Happy

Choose one of these feeling words. Looking in a full-length mirror, show that feeling through body language. Watch your face, arms, legs, and body. If you have a hard time showing some of these feelings, ask your parent or counselor to help. Practice with that person until you can show all twelve feelings with your body language.

Once you are good at showing a feeling with your body language, check it off on the list below. Keep practicing until you have checked off every one of the feeling words.

☐ Afraid	☐ Angry
☐ Interested	☐ Kind
☐ Confused	☐ Sad
☐ Embarrassed	☐ Friendly
☐ Calm	☐ Surprised
☐ Anxious	☐ Happy

The Feelings Game

Put the twelve pieces of paper in a container. On a separate piece of paper, make a list of all twelve feelings. Now you can ask your parent, your counselor, or some friends to play this game with you. Choosing a piece of paper without showing it to anyone else, each person takes a turn to act out the feeling word. The actor cannot use words or sounds, only body language. Using the list of twelve feelings, the other players try to guess the feeling being acted out. When another player guesses correctly, the actor sits down and somebody else takes a turn.

As you try out these different feelings, you will see that even when people do not use words, their faces and bodies are always "talking" to people. Sometimes, body language says that one person is friendly and likes the other person. Other times, body language seems to be saying the person is not friendly or does not like the other person. Practice friendly body language so that it gets easier and easier to do when you are around other people. People with friendly body language have more friends and more fun.

There is an old song that says, when you're smiling, the whole world smiles with you. It means that your smile is nice to see and makes everyone, including you, feel better. To start smiling at people more often, try this activity. If you are not used to smiling much, practice using a mirror. Notice how smiling changes your mouth and eyes and makes your face look friendly.

Reward Points

5 points for reading this activity
2 points for completing the blanks below the pictures
4 points for completing the checkboxes
3 points for playing the Feelings Game

Learning to Smile at Others

About This Activity

You will discover that smiling at people is a good habit you can learn by practicing. In Activity 11: Making Eye Contact, you learned to change your behavior by making a list from easiest to hardest, keeping a daily record, starting with the easiest behaviors, moving to harder behaviors when you were ready, and practicing until you had a new habit. In this activity, you will also use that important method.

On a scale from 0 to 10, rate how hard it is for you to smile at the following people. Use 0 (those it is easiest for you to smile at) and 10 (those it is hardest for you to smile at).

Adults I don't know	0	1	2	3	4	5	6	7	8	9	10
Boys who are close friends	0	1	2	3	4	5	6	7	8	9	10
Girls who are close friends	0	1	2	3	4	5	6	7	8	9	10
Teachers I know well	0	1	2	3	4	5	6	7	8	9	10
Other teachers	0	1	2	3	4	5	6	7	8	9	10
The school secretary	0	1	2	3	4	5	6	7	8	9	10
The principal of my school	0	1	2	3	4	5	6	7	8	9	10
Girls I don't know	0	1	2	3	4	5	6	7	8	9	10
Boys I don't know	0	1	2	3	4	5	6	7	8	9	10
My mother	0	1	2	3	4	5	6	7	8	9	10
My father	0	1	2	3	4	5	6	7	8	9	10
My brother(s)	0	1	2	3	4	5	6	7	8	9	10
My sisters(s)	0	1	2	3	4	5	6	7	8	9	10
Relatives I see often	0	1	2	3	4	5	6	7	8	9	10

Relatives I don't see often	0 1 2 3 4 5 6 7 8 9 10
Classmates (boys)	0 1 2 3 4 5 6 7 8 9 10
Classmates (girls)	0 1 2 3 4 5 6 7 8 9 10

Add any people in your life who are not on the list and rate them as well:

_____	0 1 2 3 4 5 6 7 8 9 10
_____	0 1 2 3 4 5 6 7 8 9 10
_____	0 1 2 3 4 5 6 7 8 9 10

Based on the ratings above, make a new list that starts with those people who seem easiest to smile at and ends with those who seem hardest to smile at.

People   **How I Rated Them**

_____   _____

_____   _____

_____   _____

_____   _____

_____   _____

_____   _____

_____   _____

_____   _____

_____   _____

People		How I Rated Them
_____		_____
_____		_____
_____		_____
_____		_____
_____		_____
_____		_____
_____		_____
_____		_____

Now you are ready to practice smiling at other people. Decide on a way to keep count of how many times you smile. However you want to keep count is okay, but here's one easy way: Put ten pennies in your pocket. Each time you smile at someone, move one of the pennies to your other pocket.

To get started, think of people from your list whom you will be seeing that day. Remember the ones who will be easiest to smile at and start with them. When you see them, make eye contact and smile. Each time you do, count that smile. See how many people you can smile at in one day. What if you are using pennies to keep count and you smile at more than ten people? Just make a note to help you remember that you already moved ten pennies, and start counting again.

Keep a daily record using the chart below:

Difficulty Level	Date	How Many People I Smiled At
0-1-2 (easy to smile at)	_____	_____
	_____	_____
	_____	_____
	_____	_____
	_____	_____
	_____	_____

Once you have practiced and are ready, move to the next level.

Difficulty Level	Date	How Many People I Smiled At
3-4 (a little harder)	_____	_____
	_____	_____
	_____	_____
	_____	_____
	_____	_____
	_____	_____

You have been practicing smiling even when it has been a little harder. When you are ready, try the next level.

Difficulty Level　　　**Date**　　　**How Many People I Smiled At**

5-6-7
(even harder)

_____　_____

_____　_____

_____　_____

_____　_____

_____　_____

By working on smiling at people, you have been acting friendlier than ever before. Things are changing for you, aren't they?

Difficulty Level　　　**Date**　　　**How Many People I Smiled At**

8-9-10
(hardest)

_____　_____

_____　_____

_____　_____

_____　_____

_____　_____

When you have practiced this part of the list, pat yourself on the back. You are doing great!

Reward Points

5 points for reading this activity and completing the rating chart
1 point for each person added to the rating chart
5 points for making the new list from easiest to hardest
2 points for each day you record smiling at people

Activity 14

When People Smile Back at You

About This Activity

You will learn that your facial expressions affect the way people act toward you and the way you feel about yourself. When you have a friendly look on your face, more people will smile at you and act friendly, and you will feel better about yourself.

Now that you are smiling at people, do they notice? If not, make eye contact and make your smile a little bigger. When you do those two things together, it is as if you were saying "I like you," and that makes people happy. They will feel like smiling back, and when they do, you will feel better about yourself. By smiling at others, you are spreading happiness. What a great thing!

In Activity 13, you kept count of how many times you smiled. In this activity, you are going to smile at people again, but you will keep count only when they smile back at you. You can use the ten-penny method to count or choose another way to keep count.

How many people can you get to smile back at you in one day? Do you think it might be two? Do you think it might be even more? Decide how many people you would like to have smile back at you in one day and write that number on the line here:

Your Goal _____

Some people might reach their goal in one day. Other people might need ten days to reach their goal. It does not matter how long it takes. The important part is that you keep smiling at people. It is important because people will start seeing that you are a friendly person, and more and more people will want to be your friend. You will not only be spreading more happiness, but will also be becoming more popular. And when you make yourself look like a happy person, you will start feeling like one.

Following is a chart to keep track of your tries until you reach your goal. You can record the number of smiles you get back each day and the new people who smile at you each day.

Date	Number of Times People Smiled Back	How Many New People Smiled Back
_____	_____	_____
_____	_____	_____
_____	_____	_____
_____	_____	_____
_____	_____	_____
_____	_____	_____
_____	_____	_____
_____	_____	_____
_____	_____	_____

Even after you reach your goal, remember to keep smiling!

Reward Points

5 points for reading this activity

2 points for each day you record how many people smile back

About This Activity

You will learn how to act confident and relaxed when you speak. When you speak in a confident, relaxed way, you are not acting shy!

People admire others who seem relaxed and confident when they speak. How do people manage to look so confident and speak so well? You can learn by carefully watching what they do. Then you will know what things to try in order to improve your speaking.

Use the chart below to record your observations of people who speak well.

Person	Makes Eye Contact	Is Easy to Hear	Smiles Often	Stands Tall with Head Up	Uses Face to Express Feelings
Newsperson on television	☐	☐	☐	☐	☐
Weatherperson on television	☐	☐	☐	☐	☐
A religious leader	☐	☐	☐	☐	☐
A favorite actor	☐	☐	☐	☐	☐
A favorite actress	☐	☐	☐	☐	☐
A favorite teacher	☐	☐	☐	☐	☐
A popular classmate	☐	☐	☐	☐	☐
The president of the United States	☐	☐	☐	☐	☐
The star of a favorite television show	☐	☐	☐	☐	☐

Look at your chart and notice how much alike these people act when they are speaking. You can learn to do these things. It just takes practice. One good way to practice is by watching yourself in a mirror as you talk. Do you smile often? Do you keep your shoulders straight and head up? Is your voice loud enough to be heard, and do you open your mouth when you speak? Does your face look friendly?

Next, you can practice speaking with a parent, counselor, or friend. As you practice, you will develop the habit of being confident and relaxed when you speak with others.

Use the chart below to record your progress. Start with a situation in which you find it easy to talk. When you are able to check off all the boxes for yourself for one situation, try a situation that is a little harder for you. With enough practice, you will be able to feel relaxed and confident when you are speaking with others.

Person	Makes Eye Contact	Is Easy to Hear	Smiles Often	Stands Tall with Head Up	Uses Face to Express Feelings
_____	☐	☐	☐	☐	☐
_____	☐	☐	☐	☐	☐
_____	☐	☐	☐	☐	☐
_____	☐	☐	☐	☐	☐
_____	☐	☐	☐	☐	☐
_____	☐	☐	☐	☐	☐
_____	☐	☐	☐	☐	☐

Reward Points
4 points for reading this activity
4 points for observing and checking boxes for at least five people
2 points each time you practice and rate yourself

About This Activity

You will feel more confident and know how good it can feel to talk with other people. You will see that fear of doing something becomes less and less strong when you do that thing over and over.

Now that you are better at smiling, this challenge will be easier. Pick someone you don't normally speak with who seems friendly or nice. It might be the librarian at school, your cousin, or the person who cuts your hair. When you see that person, use these steps to say hi or hello:

- Walk near the person and make eye contact.

- When the person looks back at you, smile.

- Say hi or hello loud enough for the person to hear you.

Practice speaking more. Start with people you see often who seem friendly. Little by little, you will get braver and braver. As you become more confident, practice greeting people you do not see as often. Use the lines below to record the times when you practice speaking more.

Date   **Who I Greeted**

_____   _____

_____   _____

_____   _____

_____   _____

_____   _____

_____   _____

_____   _____

_____   _____

_____   _____

_____   _____

Now you are ready to do even braver things, like introducing yourself and making friends.

Reward Points
3 points for reading this activity
**2 points for each date that you enter
the name of someone you greeted**

Activity 17   Meeting New People

About This Activity

You will learn and practice an important social skill: meeting people. Practicing this activity will help you gain confidence and then you will not act shy.

The best time to meet new people is when you feel relaxed and are not in a hurry. Follow these steps to introduce yourself:

- Start by picking someone whose body language is friendly.

- Take a deep breath.

- Smile and say hi or hello.

- Ask, "What's your name?" and remember the name.

- Now tell the person your name.

- Ask something you want to know about the person.

- After the person answers you, ask something else or tell something about you.

You just introduced yourself. Good for you!

Say Goodbye to Being Shy

If this activity seems hard for you, ask your parent or counselor to practice with you by acting like a person whom you want to meet. Go through the steps as many times as you need to, until you feel relaxed and confident. It will help if your parent or counselor acts like different people and gives different kinds of responses.

You can keep track of the times you meet new people by marking down the dates and tries below. You will find that the more you do this, the more relaxed and confident you will become.

Date   **Number of People I Met**

_____   _____

_____   _____

_____   _____

_____   _____

_____   _____

_____   _____

_____   _____

_____   _____

_____   _____

Reward Points

3 points for reading this activity
2 points for every completed line

> ## *About This Activity*
>
> You will learn that you can make more friends by following a few simple steps. You will also learn that it is okay when someone says no to you. Learning to accept "no" is part of saying goodbye to being shy.

Here are the steps to making new friends:

- Pick a time when you are relaxed and are not in a hurry.

- Choose someone whose body language is friendly.

- Take a deep breath.

- Smile and say hi or hello.

- Make a suggestion that starts with "Would you like to...?"

- If the answer is yes, that's great—go have fun!

- If the answer is no, try suggesting something else to do, try again later, or choose another friendly-looking person.

Start by trying to make friends with someone who seems friendly and is not too busy. Remember to smile and act friendly. Do not expect everyone to want to do what you ask. The other person might feel shy or want to be alone or have other plans. If the person says no, remind yourself that everyone gets told no at one time or another.

Here is Bill's record of the times he tried to make friends. Notice that Bill tried again even after the first person said no.

Date	What Bill Did
May 2	Asked John to swing on the swings. He said no.
May 3	Asked Madeline to play on the monkey bars. She said no and acted kind of afraid.
May 4	Asked Mark to play catch and we did.
May 4	Asked John to play on the monkey bars with Mark and me. He said he had to go inside.
	Asked Madeline to play catch. It seemed like she wanted to, but she said no. I wonder why.
May 5	Mark and I asked Madeline if she wanted to swing on the swings, and she said yes! We realized that she felt confident on the swings but not on the monkey bars or playing catch.

You can keep track of the times you try to make new friends by writing the dates and what you did here:

Date   **What I Did**

_____   _____

_____   _____

_____   _____

_____   _____

_____   _____

_____   _____

_____   _____

_____   _____

_____   _____

_____   _____

Reward Points
5 points for reading this activity
2 points for every completed line

Becoming a Better Listener

About This Activity

You will learn how much people like it when others pay attention and listen to them. You will learn to listen well and you will find that listening makes people like you.

Being a good listener is very important, but many people never learn how to do it. Listening is the way that people learn more about each other and understand each other better. Being a good listener is also a great way to make friends. Here are the steps to being a good listener:

- Sit or stand quietly.

- Make eye contact with the person who is talking.

- Think more about what the person is saying and less about what you think or feel.

- As you listen to the words, nod your head or say yes or "hmm" so the person knows you are really hearing their words.

- When the person has finished talking, ask questions to find out more.

Once you listen to people and they know that you really understand what they are saying, they will be happy to listen to you.

You can practice listening wherever you go. Each time you practice being a good listener, write the date, who was speaking, how you did, and what you can do to improve. Don't worry if you don't do very well at first. Being a good listener is hard work and takes lots of practice.

Scoring

If you interrupted a lot or did not really listen, give yourself a ☹.

If you listened to a little of what the other person said, give yourself a 😐.

If you looked at the person's face, did not interrupt, and then asked questions to find out more, give yourself a 😊.

Date	Whom I Was Listening To	How I Did	To Become a Better Listener, I Will ...
_____	_____	☺ ☺ ☹	_____
_____	_____	☺ ☺ ☹	_____
_____	_____	☺ ☺ ☹	_____
_____	_____	☺ ☺ ☹	_____
_____	_____	☺ ☺ ☹	_____
_____	_____	☺ ☺ ☹	_____
_____	_____	☺ ☺ ☹	_____
_____	_____	☺ ☺ ☹	_____
_____	_____	☺ ☺ ☹	_____
_____	_____	☺ ☺ ☹	_____
_____	_____	☺ ☺ ☹	_____
_____	_____	☺ ☺ ☹	_____
_____	_____	☺ ☺ ☹	_____
_____	_____	☺ ☺ ☹	_____

Reward Points

3 points for reading this activity

2 points for every completed line

About This Activity

You will learn how to make a good apology. When you apologize, you admit that you did something wrong, and that takes courage. A person who can offer a good apology is not acting like a shy person.

Everybody makes mistakes. Since everyone says or does the wrong thing sometimes, everyone needs to know how to apologize. Apologizing may seem hard to do at first, but as soon as you do it, you will feel better. And if the person accepts your apology, that's best of all!

Here are the steps to an apology:

- Make eye contact.

- Be sincere; act and sound like you really mean what you are saying.

- Say that what you did was wrong, without adding any excuses.

- Say that you won't do it again and really mean it.

- Ask what you could do to make the situation better.

Practice apologizing, using the scenes that follow. Have your parent or counselor practice this important skill with you. Take turns playing the part of the person who is making the apology. That way, you can find out how it feels to make an apology and also to receive an apology.

When it is your turn to practice making an apology for each scene, ask the other person to rate you on the five parts of a good apology. Talk with the person about what you can do to improve any of the parts that seem difficult. Keep practicing until you receive a check mark for all five parts.

Scene 1: Your aunt asked you not to bring your juice upstairs, but you did it anyway. The glass tipped and juice spilled on the carpet. Now you need to apologize.

- ☐ I made eye contact.
- ☐ I was sincere.
- ☐ I said that what I did was wrong and I didn't add any excuses.
- ☐ I said I wouldn't do it again and I meant it.
- ☐ I asked how I could make things better.

Scene 2: You got angry at your sister and called her a name. It is time for you to apologize.

- ☐ I made eye contact.
- ☐ I was sincere.
- ☐ I said that what I did was wrong and I didn't add any excuses.
- ☐ I said I wouldn't do it again and I meant it.
- ☐ I asked how I could make things better.

Scene 3: You borrowed your friend's CD and then lost it. You need to apologize to your friend.

- ☐ I made eye contact.
- ☐ I was sincere.
- ☐ I said that what I did was wrong and I didn't add any excuses.
- ☐ I said I wouldn't do it again and I meant it.
- ☐ I asked how I could make things better.

Now it is time to think about a real-life apology. Think of something you have done for which you should apologize, and write it here:

_____

_____

_____

_____

Practice your real-life apology and make sure you pay attention to each of the five parts. If you don't mind sharing your apology, have the person with whom you practiced rate you on the real-life apology.

In my practice apology:

☐ I made eye contact.

☐ I was sincere.

☐ I said that what I did was wrong and I didn't add any excuses.

☐ I said I wouldn't do it again and I meant it.

☐ I asked how I could make things better.

After practicing, try your real-life apology. Then rate yourself on the five parts of a good apology. If you feel you did not do well on any part, practice more with your practice partner.

In my real-life apology:

- ☐ I made eye contact.

- ☐ I was sincere.

- ☐ I said that what I did was wrong and I didn't add any excuses.

- ☐ I said I wouldn't do it again and I meant it.

- ☐ I asked how I could make things better.

The next time you make a mistake that deserves an apology, you will be able to apologize well. That is because you have practiced, developed a skill, and gained confidence. Good job!

Reward Points
5 points for reading this activity
3 points for each time you practice an apology
1 more point for each practice when the other person apologizes
5 points for each real-life apology

Happy Memories

About This Activity

You will learn that it is important to look back and think about good things from the past. When you try planning to repeat those good things, you are acting less shy and becoming more powerful. When you discuss your happy memories with other people, you will feel happy and you will help them learn more about you.

Think about some of the best things you have ever done. Some of these activities might be going on a certain vacation, getting on the honor roll at school, or teaching your dog a special trick. Write ten things you have done before and liked so much that you would like to do them again.

☐ 1. _____

☐ 2. _____

☐ 3. _____

☐ 4. _____

☐ 5. _____

☐ 6. _____

☐ 7. _____

☐ 8. _____

☐ 9. _____

☐ 10. _____

A Workbook to Help Kids Overcome Shyness

Now read your list and check the box next to the items you think you would be able to do again. Out of the activities you checked, choose one that you would not only like to do again, but could do again. For this activity, answer the questions below:

What is the activity? _____

What would you have to do to make it possible?

_____

If this activity involves others, write their names. What would they have to do to make it possible?

_____

_____

When do you think you might be able to do it again? _____

What will you do now so that you will be able to do this activity again?

_____

_____

_____

Whom do you need to talk with about doing this activity again?

_____

Reward Points
2 points for reading this activity
1 point for every item written on the list
1 point for every question answered

A Timeline of Your Accomplishments

About This Activity

You will discover that from the time you were born until now you have learned many things. Thinking about how much you have learned and the skills you have developed will give you lots of reasons to feel good about yourself.

A long time ago, you were a baby who could not do very many things at all. You could not talk or walk or even sit up. Those are all things you had to learn. Since then, you've learned many, many things. Think about it—dressing, feeding yourself, riding a bicycle, tying your shoes, and reading are all things that people learn as they get older.

Here is a timeline that shows some things one ten-year-old child has learned since birth:

10 — started to read music

9 — Learned multiplication tables, began keyboarding, started playing chess

8 — Started rollerblading, learned to count in spanish and write cursive

6 — Learned to read

5 — Learned to ride a bike, tie my shoes

4 — Started to swim

3 — Memorized the alphabet, learned to dress myself

2 — Learned to feed myself

1 — Learned to walk and talk

0 — Learned to sit up

Have some fun by making a timeline of things that you have learned since you were born. On a separate sheet of paper, make a list of those things. Next to each thing, write the age you were when you learned to do it. Put your list in order, copy it onto the lines that follow, and you will have a timeline that shows your whole life!

A Timeline of Your Accomplishments

My Timeline

Age	What I Learned to Do
_____	_____
_____	_____
_____	_____
_____	_____
_____	_____
_____	_____
_____	_____
_____	_____
_____	_____
_____	_____
_____	_____
0 _____	_____

Isn't it great to see how many things you have already learned?

Say Goodbye to Being Shy

Your Special Gifts

About This Activity

You will think about what makes you special and discover what others like about you. Doing this will help you feel more confident and capable.

Your special gifts are things you can do extra well or things about the way you look or act that people like. Your smile, the way you fix things, or your nice manners—all of these might be gifts. Do you know what your gifts are? In each gift box below, write one gift you believe you have.

Activity 23 Your Special Gifts

Now ask other people what they believe your gifts are. Do not ask just your mom or dad. Ask people like your friends, your teacher, the principal, your grandmother, your neighbor, or your school librarian. Each time someone names one of your gifts, write it in one of the gift boxes below. Keep asking until you have put one gift in each of the boxes below. You will be surprised to find out that you have more gifts than you ever imagined!

> ### *Reward Points*
> **3 points for reading this activity**
> **1 point for each box filled with a gift you believe you have**
> **3 points for each box filled with a gift other people believe you have**

A Timeline of the Future   Activity 24

About This Activity

In Activity 22: A Timeline of Your Accomplishments, you recalled some of the things you have learned since you were born. Now you are going to imagine a happy and exciting future by thinking about things you would like to learn and do from now until you turn thirty. Setting these goals is your first step to achieving them!

No matter what age people are, they can continue to learn. As you become a grownup, you will learn many new things. Becoming good at a sport, being an ice skater, speaking another language, driving a car, and dancing are all things you might learn. Think about the time from now until you are thirty years old. At the bottom of this timeline, write your current age. Then, write some of the things you would like to learn between now and when you turn thirty.

Age

30 _____

_____

_____

_____

25 _____

_____

_____

_____

Age

20 _____

_____

_____

_____

15 _____

_____

_____

_____

_____   _____

Current
Age

About This Activity

This activity shows that practice results in improved skills and abilities. By practicing and noticing improvement, you will gain a sense of control and self-confidence.

Champions are usually thought to be people like famous basketball players or football heroes. The winners of a spelling bee or a race are also called champions. They have trained and worked hard to achieve their goals. People can be champions in other ways, too. The person with a handicap who struggles just to walk a few steps is a champion, and the child who works and works until he or she can read is also a champion.

Even when people do not quite reach their goals, they can still be champions. What makes them champions? They set a positive goal and work hard to make progress. Think of all the dedicated scientists who try each day to find a cure for diseases like cancer. They have not reached their goal, but they are all champions because of their dedication and hard work.

This activity can help you see that practice will move you closer to your goals. Get an old cup (not your family's good china!) and fifty pennies. Set the cup on a rug and sit about four feet away from it. Toss the pennies one at a time and see how many you can get to stay in the cup. On the chart that follows, write the number next to Day 1, Trial #1. Do this again on Day 1 and write the second number on the line for Trial #2. Twice a day for five days, toss the fifty pennies and write how many stay in the cup. Try not to skip a day, but if you do, toss the pennies the next day.

	Trial	*Pennies in the Cup*
Day 1	Trial #1	_____
	Trial #2	_____
Day 2	Trial #3	_____
	Trial #4	_____
Day 3	Trial #5	_____
	Trial #6	_____
Day 4	Trial #7	_____
	Trial #8	_____
Day 5	Trial #9	_____
	Trial #10	_____

Did you get more pennies in the cup on your tenth try than you did on your first try? Your improvement is an example of how any skill will improve with practice. Remember that practice and hard work will make you a champion.

The next part of this activity involves hard exercise, so make sure your parent says it is okay for you to do it.

Many professional athletes and almost all boxers train by jumping rope. Get a jump rope that turns easily and has good grips. Ask someone to keep time for you or set a timer for three minutes and count how many times you jump the rope in three minutes. If you miss, that's okay. Just keep jumping and counting, but do not start over at zero. The idea is to see how many jumps you can do in three minutes. Try to do this for ten days in a row. If you miss a day, just do it the next day until you have done it for ten days. Record your jumps on the chart that follows.

Day	Number of Jumps in Three Minutes
1	_____
2	_____
3	_____
4	_____
5	_____
6	_____
7	_____
8	_____
9	_____
10	_____

Unless you are already a jump-rope professional, you will see a big increase in the number of jumps from Day 1 to Day 10. You might even want to continue jumping rope every day—it is great exercise! As you get better at it, you will prove to yourself that you can train to be a champion.

Now that you know how to train, you can pick any skill that you want to become better at. Figure out a schedule that will give you lots of practice and a way to keep a record of your progress. For example, if you chose shooting baskets, you could write the number of baskets you make; if you chose playing the piano, you could write how many songs you play well. On the lines below, write the skill you want to improve and how you will measure your progress.

The skill I want to improve is _____.

I will measure my progress by _____.
                                    (counting, measuring, timing, etc.)

Day	Record of Progress
1	_____
2	_____
3	_____
4	_____
5	_____
6	_____
7	_____
8	_____
9	_____
10	_____

You can make additional charts to keep up this training or add a new skill to practice. Congratulations—now you know that you can train to be a champion!

> ### *Reward Points*
> **5 points for reading this activity**
> **2 points for each time you practice tossing pennies**
> **2 points for every day you jump rope**
> **2 points for each day you practice another skill**
> **2 extra points for every day you practice that skill for more than twenty minutes**

About This Activity

You will learn that practice and work can lead to improved self-confidence. One way to build self-confidence is to become better at something you can already do. Another way is to develop a completely new skill.

In this activity, you will boost your self-confidence by selecting two hobbies or skills to develop. One should be something you already do but want to do more often or do better. The other hobby or skill should be something you have always wanted to do but have never tried.

You will have more fun if you choose activities you can share, so select activities that involve other people. Below are some ideas, and you can use the blank lines to add your own.

Art lessons	Swimming
Tennis	Gymnastics
Golf	Chess
Bowling	Singing in a choir
Dance lessons	Planting a garden
Karate	Making cookies

_____

_____

_____

_____

After your list is complete, show it to your parent or counselor. Choose an activity you have done and would like to do more often or better. Then, choose an activity you have never done but would like to try. Decide on activities you will be able to do on a regular basis.

This is the activity I have done before and want to do more often or better:

_____.

This is the new activity I would like to try:

_____.

Figure out a schedule for these activities and a way to keep a record of your progress.

For example, if you are running, you could write how long you ran before getting tired. If you are knitting, you could write how much you knitted and how it came out. If you are not sure how to record your progress, ask your parent or counselor for help. Before you start recording your progress, make copies of the record below so you can continue to keep track.

Date	Record of Progress
_____	_____
_____	_____
_____	_____
_____	_____
_____	_____
_____	_____
_____	_____
_____	_____
_____	_____

Date	Record of Progress
_____	_____
_____	_____
_____	_____
_____	_____
_____	_____
_____	_____
_____	_____

Have fun with your old and new activities! If you ever become discouraged about your progress, think about these old sayings:

Practice makes perfect.
What it means: it takes lots of practice to become really good at something.

The longest journey begins with a single step.
What it means: to get somewhere that seems far away, you must get started and stick to your plan.

Reward Points
5 points for reading this activity and selecting activities to do (earned only the first time)

2 points earned each time you participate in one of the selected activities and write down what you did

---

How People Show They Care

About This Activity

You will think about all the help you get from others, which lets you know that all around you are people who care for you and love you. When you think about this, you will feel more secure and confident.

Think about some of the things that people do for you. Write the names of the people who do these things on the lines below. If it is more than one person, either write the person who does it most or write all the names. On the blank lines at the end of this activity, you can add other things that people do for you and the names of the people who do them.

_____ washes my clothes.

_____ helps me learn at school.

_____ gives me treats.

_____ cares for me when I'm sick.

_____ cooks food for me.

_____ takes me to fun places.

_____ gets me to school.

_____ takes care of my teeth.

_____ makes me laugh.

_____ drives me to appointments.

_____ shows me how to play sports.

_____ helps me with homework.

_____ hugs me.

_____ plays games with me.

_____

_____

_____

_____

_____

_____

_____

Reward Points
3 points for reading this activity
5 points for filling in as many lines as you can
2 points for each extra helping activity you add to the list

About This Activity

You will have a chance to think about the people who care for you and love you. When you are thinking about people who help and are feeling grateful for them, you are not thinking the thoughts that go with acting shy.

Isn't it amazing to think about all the people who help you? It's a great thing that there are so many people who care about you. Every time people do something for you, they are using their actions to let you know that you are special to them. When you are having a tough day, think about these people.

Who is the person who helps you the most? Write that person's name here:

_____

Think for a minute and write the most important thing, or things, this person does for you:

_____

_____

_____

_____

_____

Now think about something you can do to help someone else. Maybe you can do one of your mom's chores or help your dad without being asked. Maybe you can help someone at school or in your neighborhood. Write down the dates and what you did to help.

Date   **What I Did to Help**

_____   _____

_____   _____

_____   _____

_____   _____

_____   _____

_____   _____

_____   _____

_____   _____

Reward Points
3 points for reading this activity
1 point for naming a person who helps you
3 points for each time you help someone else

A Workbook to Help Kids Overcome Shyness

About This Activity

You will have the chance to thank someone who is special to you. When you thank others, they feel good and you have done something nice. When you act nice, you also feel good about yourself.

People need each other. Many other people help you, and it is important to thank them often. When you thank others, you do something that makes them happy, and you make yourself feel happy by doing it.

Think of someone who might like to get a thank-you note from you. Write a note or make a card. Be sure to write why you are saying thanks. You can deliver it or mail it. The person will be happy to get such a nice note from you and may even keep it forever!

Reward Points

3 points for reading this activity

**6 points for writing a note or making a card
and giving it to the person**

Expressing Yourself "Just Right"

About This Activity

You will learn how to be assertive, which means telling someone what you want without being too forceful or not forceful enough. Being assertive means you are not acting shy.

Do you remember the story of Goldilocks and the Three Bears? When Goldilocks went into the bears' home, she found three bowls of porridge—one that was too hot, one that was too cold, and one that was just right. Then she found three chairs—one that was too big, one that was too small, and one that was just right.

"Just right" is important. Shoes should not be too loose or too tight; they should be just right. Bath water should not be too cold or too hot; it needs to be just right. A dog should not be fed too little or too much; the amount needs to be just right. Here is another example of "just right":

Pretend that you are at a restaurant and want to order a grilled-cheese sandwich. When the waiter asks what you want, if you:

- Say nothing at all or speak too quietly to be heard, that is too weak.

- Scream, "I WANT GRILLED CHEESE NOW," that is too tough.

- Look at the waiter and say, "I would like a grilled-cheese sandwich, please," that is just right.

Now it's your turn. Read the example below and check the box for the answer that is just right.

You are on the playground, and someone from your class asks if you would like to play kickball. You don't want to play, so you:

☐ Don't answer and just look away.

☐ Look grouchy and say, "Leave me alone!"

☐ Look friendly and say, "No, thanks."

Did you choose to look friendly and say, "No, thanks"? That is the "just right" answer. When you are asked a question or would like to tell somebody what you want, follow these three steps to say it just right:

1. Make eye contact with the person.

2. Use a clear voice that is loud enough for the other person to hear.

3. Use "please" and "thank you."

Practice being assertive when answering and asking questions with your parent or counselor. After each question, ask the other person to rate you on doing it just right. Talk with your parent or counselor about what you can do to improve any step you find difficult. Practice until you receive a check for all three steps.

Answer the following: would you like eggs or cereal for breakfast?

☐ When I answered, I made eye contact.

☐ I used a clear voice, loud enough to be heard.

☐ I used "please."

Practice saying yes to this question: would you like to play Monopoly now?

☐ When I answered yes, I made eye contact.

☐ I used a clear voice, loud enough to be heard.

☐ I used "please."

Now practice saying no to the question about Monopoly.

☐ When I answered no, I made eye contact.

☐ I used a clear voice, loud enough to be heard.

☐ I used "thank you."

Pretend that you are at your grandmother's house and you are asking her for something to drink.

☐ When I asked, I made eye contact.

☐ I used a clear voice, loud enough to be heard.

☐ I used "please."

Pretend that you are at a new friend's house and need to use the bathroom. Practice asking your friend about using the bathroom.

☐ When I asked, I made eye contact.

☐ I used a clear voice, loud enough to be heard.

☐ I used "please."

Now think of a real-life situation where you could do a better job of being assertive. It might be talking in a restaurant, asking your teacher for help, or joining a group. With a partner, practice until you are confident you can handle the situation just right, and then try it in real life.

After you have been assertive in the real-life situation, rate yourself on the three steps.

My real-life situation: _____

☐ I made eye contact.

☐ I used a clear voice, loud enough to be heard.

☐ I used "please" and "thank you."

Keep practicing being a "just right" assertive person. This is a big step toward saying goodbye to being shy.

Reward Points
5 points for reading this activity
2 points for each time you practiced being assertive
5 points for being assertive in a real-life situation and rating yourself

---

Activity 31　　　Teasing Is Not Pleasing

Have you ever been teased? If you asked all the grownups and kids you know, probably every one of them would tell you that they have been teased. Teasing is never fun. It is annoying and it hurts people's feelings. It is important to remember not to tease other people and it is important to know what you can do if people start teasing you. Here are some ideas.

Try Being a Broken Record

Years ago, people did not play music on CDs. Instead, they played music on records. When a record was broken, it would play the same part over and over again. In this cartoon, Louis is acting like a broken record by saying the same sentence again and again.

If you want to act like a broken record when someone starts to tease you, pick one thing to say that is not mean and then calmly say it over and over. Usually, the person will get tired of teasing and stop.

Get ready to practice being a broken record by writing your own script. Choose a sentence that is comfortable to you, and write it on each of the blank lines below. Ask your parent or counselor pretend to be a teasing child so you can rehearse being a broken record.

Parent or counselor: Hey, that was a really stupid thing you did!

You: _____

Parent or counselor: It was stupid, and so are you!

You: _____

Parent or counselor: I said it was stupid, and now you're acting stupid!

You: _____

Parent or counselor: Whatever! (ends teasing)

Practice this until you are good at being a broken record.

Try Ignoring

Ignoring means pretending that you did not even hear the mean thing the other person said. Look at how Jenny ignores teasing:

Have your parent or counselor pretend to be teasing you so that you can practice ignoring. Your parent can use the same words from the last practice or make up new teasing comments. Practice until you are good at ignoring teasing.

Try Changing the Subject

Changing the subject is fun to try. You pick one thing to talk about, and you just keep talking about that one thing, no matter what the other person says. See how Adam changes the subject by talking about his video game.

When you change the subject, sometimes the person will stop teasing. Sometimes, the teaser will even start to talk about what you're talking about!

Have your parent or counselor pretend to tease you so that you can practice changing the subject. He or she can use the words from the first practice or make up new teasing comments. Practice until you are good at changing the subject.

Once you have practiced being a broken record, ignoring, and changing the subject, it will be easy for you to decide which ways work best for you to handle teasing. What do you think you will do the next time somebody starts teasing?

Write it here: _____

_____

Here is something important to remember: Being a broken record, ignoring, and changing the subject are three great ways to try to get somebody to stop teasing. However, if somebody keeps teasing anyway or tries to touch you or your things, tell an adult right away.

> ### *Reward Points*
> **5 points for reading this activity**
> **3 points each time you practice a teasing scene**

About This Activity

You will learn how to stop bullies, either by yourself or by finding an adult who can help. Taking action to stop bullying is not acting shy!

Bullies hurt or scare other people on purpose, not just once but many times. There are different ways that people can be bullies. They can use their bodies by pushing, hitting, kicking, or spitting on another person. They can also use words to threaten, say mean things, or spread rumors about someone. They can get others to be mean to the person they are bullying and to keep that person out of the group.

Here are five things you can do if someone is bullying you:

1. **Tell an adult.**
   You don't have to handle a bully by yourself. If the first adult you tell does not do anything to help, tell another adult.

   Practice: Pretend you are being bullied at school. Whom would you tell? Have your parent or counselor pretend to be the adult you would tell. Practice what you would say as you discuss the bullying with an adult.

2. **Stay with a buddy.**
   It is easier to bully someone who is alone. When you are with a friend, you have someone who can help.

   Practice: When are you likely to be bullied? Is there someone who could be with you when you might be bullied? Discuss this with your parent or counselor.

3. **Ignore the bully.**
   Bullies who are ignored sometimes get bored and stop their bullying. Try to walk away calmly. If the bully tries to stop you, tell an adult.

   Practice: You may have practiced ignoring in Activity 31: Teasing Is Not Pleasing. This time, practice again while your parent or counselor acts even meaner. Discuss what you can do if the bully gets more and more mean as you ignore him or her.

4. **Use brave body language.**

   When you act afraid or sad, it might make the bully feel like acting even meaner. Act brave instead—hold your head up, stand straight, and walk confidently. Bullies often pick on people who look afraid, so no matter how you feel, act brave.

   Practice: Practice standing and walking while you use brave body language. Ask your parent or counselor for suggestions about how to look confident. Practice each suggestion until you can do it well without thinking.

5. **Use assertive language, but be respectful.**

   Even when a bully is being mean, don't be mean back. Just say firmly, "I don't like it when you do that. Please stop now."

   Practice: Ask your parent or counselor to act like a bully. Practice what you would say to tell the bully to stop. Ask your parent or counselor what you can do to improve your response to the bully. Practice until you can do it well.

When you do these things, most people will stop bullying and start acting kinder. But if a person keeps bullying, keep on telling others until you are helped and the bullying stops.

Reward Points

5 points for reading this activity

2 points each time you practice one of the suggested responses with your parent or counselor

---

Say Goodbye to Being Shy

Using Positive Self-Talk   Activity 33

About This Activity

You will learn how to send yourself positive messages rather than putting yourself down. Using positive self-talk will increase your feelings of self-worth. It is an important step in overcoming anxiety or feelings of shyness.

To "move mountains" is to do something that makes a big difference. By doing this activity, you will start to change how you think. As you change how you think, you will change the way you feel about yourself, and that will move mountains in your life.

People's thoughts often include self-talk, the comments they make about themselves inside their heads. Many people think mean things about themselves. When their self-talk is mean, people may start to feel bad about themselves, and they may not like themselves as much as they should.

Below are put-downs some people say to themselves. Circle the ones you have thought about yourself.

I'm stupid.	That was dumb.
Nobody likes me.	I'm ugly.
People think I look funny.	I can't do anything right.
I'm too short.	I'm too tall.
I sound funny.	My hair is ugly.
My ears are too big.	My smile is funny.
I'm fat.	I'm skinny.
I'm weak.	I'm clumsy.
I'm a sissy.	I don't have any friends.

Are there other mean things you say to yourself? Write them here:_____

_____

These put-downs or bad thoughts make us feel sad, afraid, and upset. When you think these thoughts, it always makes things worse, but you can train yourself to break this hurtful habit.

Every time you catch yourself thinking a mean thought, tell yourself, "Forget putting myself down. I'll do something positive." Or pretend you have a traffic policeman in your head who says, "Stop! That is not allowed here," when he or she sees a put-down coming.

Practice with different ways to stop put-down thoughts. When you find one you like, write it below.

My put-down stopper is:

_____

If put-downs and bad thoughts are not allowed, your brain needs something else to do. So think good thoughts about yourself! Below are some examples of positive self-talk. Circle the ones you would like to believe about yourself.

I'm smart.	I'm kind to people.
People like me.	I'm respectful.
I'm a good singer.	I'm a good sport.
I'm a hard worker.	People can count on me.
I eat healthy food.	I exercise every day.
I help other people.	I'm good at soccer.
I try to do the right thing.	I'm clean and neat.
I'm a good cook.	I smile a lot.
I'm a good swimmer.	I care about people.

What other good things can you say to yourself?

_____

_____

By practicing positive self-talk, you can make it a habit. Here is one way to get used to getting rid of put-downs and using positive self-talk instead.

Start each day with ten pennies in your pocket. Every time you think a good thought about yourself, move one penny to your other pocket. When you catch yourself having mean thoughts about yourself, move a penny back to the first pocket. If you move all the pennies to the "good" pocket, make a note that you have moved ten pennies and start over again. See how many pennies you can move to the "good" pocket. Keep a daily record by using the chart below:

Date   **Number of Pennies in the "Good" Pocket**

_____   _____

_____   _____

_____   _____

_____   _____

_____   _____

_____   _____

_____   _____

_____   _____

_____   _____

_____   _____

> ### *Reward Points*
> **6 points for reading this activity**
> **2 points for circling the put-downs**
> **2 points for every extra put-down you write**
> **2 points for a put-down stopper**
> **2 points for circling the good thoughts**
> **2 points for every extra good thought you write**
> **2 points for every day you record moving pennies**

It may not seem to make a big difference at first, but keep trying. Every day, it will get a little easier to think more and more good things about yourself. By thinking more good things about yourself every day, you will start to believe these good things. You will be moving mountains!

Activity 34   Focusing on Good Things

About This Activity

You will learn that when people think about good things that happen, they have less time to think about sad or bad things. And the more they think about good things, the more good things they notice. Focusing on good things can help you stop acting shy.

Every day, write down the three best things that happened that day. As you start making this a habit, you will like what happens.

1. You will start looking for, and finding, more happy things.

2. You will feel better inside because you are spending extra time thinking about good things.

3. Because you are feeling better, others will feel happy being with you.

Date   **The Three Best Things That Happened Today**

_____   _____

                  _____

                  _____

_____   _____

                  _____

                  _____

_____   _____

                  _____

                  _____

Date	The Three Best Things That Happened Today
____	_____
	_____
	_____
____	_____
	_____
	_____
____	_____
	_____
	_____

Writing down the three best things that happen every day is a great habit, so don't stop once these lines are filled. You can continue in a notebook or journal. You will be creating a list of good things that will grow longer and longer. When you are having a sad or bad day, read your list. When you remember all the good things that have happened, you will feel better!

> ### *Reward Points*
> **3 points for reading this activity**
> **1 point for every good thing written**

About This Activity

You will learn that when you look for friendliness, you will find it. By noticing people who are kind and friendly, you will gain confidence and not act shy.

Sometimes people act shy because they think that other people do not like them, are judging them, or are making fun of them. They might remember times when someone ignored them or was not kind to them, and they make the mistake of thinking that many people will act that way. That makes it easy to feel sad or scared and to keep acting shy for a long time.

But here's the good news: There are many kind and friendly people, and you can train yourself to notice them. By doing this, it will get easier and easier to notice friendly actions when they happen. It will become easier for you to feel happy more often. When you feel happy and notice more kind and friendly people, you will gain confidence and not act shy.

It is time to play detective and look for the kind, friendly things that people in your life are doing. Here are some of those things:

- Smiling at you

- Waving at you

- Complimenting you

- Patting your shoulder

- Asking you to play

- Looking at you in a friendly way

- Listening to you

- Asking you a friendly question

- Helping you

- Giving you something

- Holding a door for you

- Asking for your ideas

- Asking for your help

What are some ways that people have shown friendliness to you? List them here:

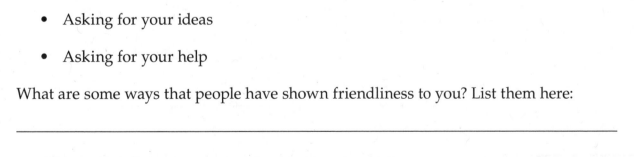

_____

_____

_____

Now it's time to practice looking for signs of friendliness. For ten days, count the signs of friendliness you notice. You can use pennies to keep count, like you did in earlier activities, or you can use your own favorite way. Remember that it's okay to encourage friendliness by sending your own friendly signals, like waving, smiling, and making eye contact.

Day	Number of Friendly Signs	Who Gave These Signs	
1	_____	_____	_____
		_____	_____
2	_____	_____	_____
		_____	_____
3	_____	_____	_____
		_____	_____
4	_____	_____	_____
		_____	_____
5	_____	_____	_____
		_____	_____
6	_____	_____	_____
		_____	_____

7 _____ _____ _____
_____ _____

8 _____ _____ _____
_____ _____

9 _____ _____ _____
_____ _____

10 _____ _____ _____
_____ _____

> ### *Reward Points*
> **3 points for reading this activity**
> **2 points for listing ways people show friendliness**
> **2 points for each day you record friendly signs**

About This Activity

You will learn that it is harmful to compare yourself to other people. If you practice thinking positively about how you are doing rather worrying about who is "the best," you will feel better about yourself.

Almost everyone dislikes being compared to someone else. "Why can't you be like your sister or brother?" are words that no one likes to hear. Even so, people often do it to themselves.

People are likely to compare themselves to someone who is better at something. Instead of thinking, "I am getting better at jumping rope," they think, "Dion is better at jumping rope than I am." Putting themselves down causes them to feel bad. They may avoid doing things and sometimes even give up.

You can train yourself to avoid negative comparisons and bad feelings, and to build yourself up and increase good feelings. In each situation below, when Ramon compares himself to someone else, he feels worse. When he uses positive thoughts, he feels better and will keep trying.

What happened: Ramon finished second in a race.

What happened: Ramon got a C+ on a test.

Now read the situations that follow. Imagine what Ramon thought or felt, and write your ideas in the spaces below.

What happened: Susan picked José as her reading partner instead of Ramon.

Ramon will feel that nobody likes him if he thinks a put-down thought

like: _____.

Ramon will feel better if he thinks:_____.

What happened: Ramon did six chin-ups. Rocky did eleven chin-ups.

If Ramon thinks a put-down thought like, "Rocky did five more chin-ups than I did. I must be weak," Ramon will feel:

_____.

Ramon will feel better if he thinks:_____.

Can you see how comparing yourself to someone else is harmful, while positive thoughts are helpful? Practice using positive thoughts instead of negative comparisons for things that have happened in your life.

What happened: _____

Your positive thought: _____

_____

How you felt: _____

_____

What happened: _____

Your positive thought: _____

_____

How you felt: _____

_____

What happened: _____

Your positive thought: _____

_____

How you felt: _____

_____

Reward Points

5 points for reading this activity

2 points for filling in the blanks in each of the "Ramon" exercises

2 points for your responses in each of the "What Happened" sections

---

What's the Worst That Could Happen?

About This Activity

You will learn that most of the things that people worry about are not as bad as they imagine. When you learn to think in a positive way, you will be able to worry less. Then you will feel happier and act less shy.

Many people worry too much. They waste time each day thinking that something bad might happen and ask themselves questions like these:

- What if I stammer when I talk?
- What if I trip and fall?
- What if the other kids don't like me?
- What if no one sits with me at lunch?
- What if I ask a question and people laugh?

In this activity, you have the chance to do something that is really fun: you get to make mistakes on purpose! By making mistakes on purpose, you will find that the worst that could happen is not as bad as you think. Here are some ideas:

1. When you speak to someone, get mixed up on purpose. For example, when you see your teacher, say, "Good teacher, morning" instead of, "Good morning, teacher." Or if your mom has a rose say, "That's a nice nose, Mom" instead of saying, "That's a nice rose, Mom." Practice how you will say your mixed-up speech so it comes out naturally. After your speech mistake, see if you can laugh about it. Follow up by saying something like, "Wow, I mixed that up! I meant to say...." You can try doing it with two different people and compare how they react.

2. Using a notebook with loose papers in it, practice at home so that you can drop the notebook and have the papers scatter. Then at school or some other public place, drop your notebook while you are walking. Pick a time and place that will not cause a lot of trouble. Some people will ignore what happened. Others might try to help you

pick up the papers. Do this in front of two different groups of people. Think to yourself, "Everyone makes mistakes. What's the worst that can happen?"

3. With your parent's permission, find an unusual way to wear your clothing in public. You might choose to wear two different socks or shoes that do not match. You could decide to wear your shirt or jacket inside out or backward. You will find that many people do not even seem to notice that you are wearing something strange. If somebody does say something, you can answer, "I guess this does look weird" or "You know, this looked a lot better this morning!" Try wearing something unusual two times. See if you can have fun and laugh about it.

You can also think up your own ideas of mistakes to try on purpose. Whatever you decide to do, try it twice and write about it below.

What you said or did: _____

Did you laugh about it?   ☐ Yes   ☐ No

How the other person or people acted: _____

_____

What you said or did: _____

Did you laugh about it?   ☐ Yes   ☐ No

How the other person or people acted: _____

_____

Now you have learned that if you accept mistakes as a part of life, you can handle them in a positive way. Remember, how you look at or think about something affects your feelings and your behavior, so it is very important to be positive. If you start to worry about making mistakes, remember to ask yourself, "What's the worst that could happen?"

Reward Points

5 points for reading this activity

**3 points for each time you practice making a
mistake and write it down**

Say Goodbye to Being Shy

Becoming a Leader

About This Activity

You will learn that by not acting shy, you are becoming a person who can do great things. You will gain the confidence, skills, and tools that can turn you into a leader.

Look at the sentences below. Which of them describe ways that you have changed since you started doing the activities in this book? If shyness is not a big problem anymore, many of these statements could be true for you. Read the sentences and check the box that describes how you are doing at this time.

	Need More Practice	Making Progress	Doing Okay
I know how to make myself feel calmer and more relaxed.	☐	☐	☐
I know how important it is to think positive thoughts.	☐	☐	☐
I know that when I practice something, I will get better at it and it will become easier to do well.	☐	☐	☐
I can think of many things I do well.	☐	☐	☐
I can handle my mistakes without putting myself down.	☐	☐	☐
I know what kinds of things I might like to do in the future.	☐	☐	☐
I am acting friendlier with other people.	☐	☐	☐
I am noticing more friendly people now.	☐	☐	☐

A Workbook to Help Kids Overcome Shyness

Becoming a Leader

	Need More Practice	Making Progress	Doing Okay
I know that heroes do the right thing even when it is hard for them.	☐	☐	☐
I am doing more good deeds for other people.	☐	☐	☐
I know how to handle teasing and bullying.	☐	☐	☐
I notice many nice or happy things that happen each day.	☐	☐	☐
I feel braver than I did when I first started the activities in this book.	☐	☐	☐
I have made at least one new friend.	☐	☐	☐

Now that you have started making changes, and shyness is less of a problem for you, you are doing things that will make you a leader. As you do more of these things, you will become more of a leader.

Reward Points
5 points for reading this activity and completing the checklist

---

Learning by Teaching

About This Activity

One good way to learn to do something well is by teaching it to someone else. This activity focuses on important lessons you have learned. By sharing what you have learned with others, you will help other people and learn it better yourself.

You have learned many things by doing the activities in this book. Teaching someone else what you have learned is a good way for you to learn it even better and to remember it. Whom could you teach? Perhaps you have a younger brother, a sister, or a close friend who can learn from you. You could teach them by telling and showing them how you learned to change your actions. For example, your younger sister may not know how to answer the telephone. You could teach her what to do in a pretend phone call and practice with her. When she feels confident, you can have her answer a real call, using the skills she has learned from you.

To whom can you teach a new skill?

_____

What can you teach that person?

_____

_____

What did you learn when you taught the new skill?

_____

_____

Just as many people help you, it is important for you to help others learn what you know about becoming braver and being less afraid. Here are some ways you can help:

- When someone in class at school seems too shy to read or answer questions, tell the person that you know he or she can do it.

- If someone in your class at school has trouble doing schoolwork in a subject you are good at, ask the teacher if you can help.

- When somebody is alone on the playground or in the lunchroom and needs a friend, ask if that person would like to play or talk.

- When you see someone who seems shy, try smiling and saying hello. Don't be surprised if the person does not answer right away. Just keep smiling and saying hi each time you have a chance. If you keep doing it, the person who is feeling shy will start to believe that you are a very nice person—and you will be. One day, the shy person might even answer you and smile back!

Write a description below of times when you have tried to help someone:

1. _____

_____

_____

2. _____

_____

_____

3. _____

_____

_____

4. _____

_____

_____

5. _____

_____

_____

6. _____

_____

_____

7. _____

_____

_____

8. _____

_____

_____

Reward Points

5 points for reading this activity

10 points for answering the three questions and trying to teach someone a new skill

3 points for each written response telling how you tried to help someone

A Workbook to Help Kids Overcome Shyness

Activity 40   Checking Your Progress

About This Activity

You will develop the habit of checking your behavior on a regular basis. Checking regularly will help you to maintain the positive behaviors you have learned.

People who act shy often avoid social situations. They may be afraid of failing or of being embarrassed, or they may want to avoid unhappy feelings or thoughts they have had in the past. Avoiding social situations is harmful because it keeps them from the very things they need—more experience, more practice, and more success with social behavior.

When a car is new or has just been repaired, it runs smoothly. After a while, parts may wear out or the car may not run smoothly because of other problems. When this happens, the car may need a tune-up.

Just as cars can be checked to find out if they need tune-ups, you can check your behavior to find out how you are doing. In this book, you have learned and practiced many social behaviors. Are you still doing all the wonderful things you have learned and practiced, or do you need a tune-up?

Rate yourself on the following behaviors. If your rating is in the "time for a tune-up" range, you can review the activity you need and practice more. Every two months, look over this list to find out if you need a tune-up.

Say Goodbye to Being Shy

Step One

Get a calendar for the year ahead and put it where you will see it every day. Circle today's date and the date every two months for the next year.

Step Two

Circle the number that describes how you think you are doing on the following social behaviors:

Behavior	Time for a Tune-Up			Could Improve			Doing It Well			
Making eye contact (Activity 11: Making Eye Contact)	0	1	2	3	4	5	6	7	8	9	10
Using positive body language (Activity 12: Body Language)	0	1	2	3	4	5	6	7	8	9	10
Smiling (Activity 13: Learning to Smile at Others)	0	1	2	3	4	5	6	7	8	9	10
Using relaxed, confident speech (Activity 15: Speaking with Confidence)	0	1	2	3	4	5	6	7	8	9	10
Greeting people (Activity 16: Don't Act Shy—Say Hi!)	0	1	2	3	4	5	6	7	8	9	10
Trying to meet people (Activity 17: Meeting New People)	0	1	2	3	4	5	6	7	8	9	10
Talking to people (Activity 18: Making Friends)	0	1	2	3	4	5	6	7	8	9	10

Step Three

For every behavior in the "time for a tune-up" range, review the activity you did earlier. Practice the behavior until it becomes a habit that you do every day.

Step Four

Every two months on the dates you marked on your calendar, check your behavior. This self-check will help you make sure that you keep practicing your positive behaviors.

Reward Points

3 points for reading this activity

5 points for completing the ratings

5 points for every two-month check

** For every activity you practice, also give yourself
the points indicated on that activity page.**

Planning for Next Year   Activity 41

About This Activity

You will set goals for the year ahead and develop a plan to work toward those goals. Preparing yourself with a plan can help you keep from acting shy.

Isn't it wonderful that you can do so many things that used to be hard? What will you do to become even braver, stronger, and more skilled? Use the space below to plan ahead for next year.

I am _____ years old. A year from now, I will be _____ years old.

A year from now, here is what I would like to be doing differently in my family:

_____

_____

Here are the changes I would like to see with my friendships by next year:

_____

_____

These are the changes I would like to see in my schoolwork next year:

_____

_____

In a year, these are the activities I would like to be doing in school:

_____

_____

Now that you have been thinking about the future, it is time to plan how you will make these changes happen.

What can you start doing in your family now?

_____

_____

What can you start doing now to make the changes with friends that you would like?

_____

_____

As you think about the changes you want to see in your schoolwork, what could you start doing now so that these changes will come true?

_____

_____

When you think about the school activities you would like to be doing next year, what is the best thing you could start doing now?

_____

_____

Reward Points
2 points for reading this activity and filling in the ages
2 points for each written answer

Say Goodbye to Being Shy

About This Activity

You will have a chance to think about the progress you have made since starting the activities in this book. You can feel good about how far you have come!

Remember how big the shyness was when you started the activities in this book? Look back to Activity 3: What Does Your Shyness Feel Like? and notice how big your shyness felt. If you have been doing the exercises in this book and your shyness feels very small or is gone, it is time for you to do this activity. If shyness is still a problem for you, go back over the activities that you know will help you the most. When you have decided that shyness is a very small problem or not a problem at all, draw a picture of you and the shyness in the box below.

Now add today's date so you will know when you drew this picture: _____

Why do you think the shyness is now less of a problem or not a problem at all?

_____

_____

What are you doing, or have you done, differently?

_____

_____

Which of your actions have helped the most?

_____

_____

Who has helped you the most? Remember to say thanks!

_____

If you ever feel shyness becoming a problem again, remember that you have learned ways to help yourself. The five-step system used in Activities 11 and 13 is the same system you can use anytime you want to change your behavior.

Fill in the blanks below to remind yourself of the five steps:

1. Make a list from _____ to _____.

2. Keep a daily _____.

3. Start with the _____ behavior.

4. When you are ready, try the behavior that is one level _____.

5. Practice until you have formed a new _____.

> ### *Reward Points*
> **3 points for reading this activity**
> **3 points for drawing**
> **1 point for answering each question**
> **2 points for filling in all five steps**

Richard Brozovich, Ph.D., is a certified school psychologist and licensed psychologist in the state of Michigan. He has worked with children in schools and private practice for more than forty years. Brozovich has a special interest in anxious and shy children and has extensive experience with children who are selectively mute. He has authored and co-authored publications about children in foster care, learning disabilities, attention deficit disorder, and school resources. For the past ten years, he has written a weekly newspaper column about school-related issues and the field of psychology. In 2003, Brozovich was selected by his colleagues to be Michigan's School Psychologist of the Year.

Linda Chase, LMSW, is an elementary school social worker. She has also worked as a psychotherapist specializing in children and family issues. Chase has co-authored books on the subjects of foster children and selective mutism and presents workshops for children and parents on various topics including life skills, communication, and problem solving.

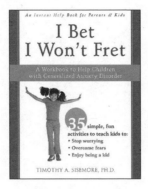
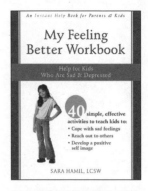

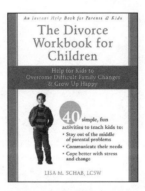